Feb 2, 1986

To Ken & Cathy,

Thanks for taking care
of our little "CARE BEAR". WE
love you and thank God for your
stands upon His mighty WORD

XXXX
OOOO
Tom & Laurie

Life Lines

Dr. Victor Paul Wierwille

Life Lines

Quotations
of
Victor Paul Wierwille

American Christian Press

International Standard Book Number 0-910068-64-X
Library of Congress Catalog Card Number 85-52028
American Christian Press
The Way International
New Knoxville, Ohio 45871
© 1985 by The Way International
First Edition 1985. First Printing 1985
Printed in the United States of America

CONTENTS

FOREWORD

Over the years, Dr. Wierwille expressed great admiration for the writing style of Mr. E.W. Kenyon. Referring to such works as *Jesus the Healer* or *The Father and His Family*, he said to me more than once that Kenyon wrote the way he had learned to teach—with succinct, power-packed statements that summed up great truth in a brief manner.

Dr. Wierwille admired the statements and writings of the great American humorist Will Rogers, as well. Rogers also manifested this unique and disciplined communication skill. I recall sitting in an airplane with Dr. Wierwille as he went through one of Rogers' books that I had given him. We talked, laughed, and reveled in the logical, penetrating, and humorous ways Rogers expressed himself.

At perhaps the other end of the spectrum, yet having similar traits of communication ability, was the American philosopher Ralph Waldo Emerson. I recall several occasions on which Dr. Wierwille read Emerson to a few of us who were traveling with him or to a roomful of Way Corps students. Although not always agreeing with his conclusions, Dr. Wierwille enjoyed Emerson's vocabulary and skills in written communication.

Pithy, succinct, crystallized statements of depth and resonance were not only admired by Dr. Wierwille, but utilized and developed. He developed the art form of teaching with that style—not generalizing, but speaking to the core of an issue of truth in a vocabulary and manner that encouraged the listener to savor, decide, believe, act, and understand. We are proud to present a representative sampling of the *Life Lines* of this master teacher.

L. Craig Martindale
December 1985

PREFACE

In September of 1984, Dr. Victor Paul Wierwille made a single-sentence suggestion to Rev. L. Craig Martindale while they were flying home to The Way International Headquarters on *Ambassador One:* "Maybe you ought to think about putting a book together, son, made up of short statements I've spoken over the years which have blessed people." That was the end of the subject. The two men, the Founding President and the President of The Way International never spoke of it again.

The preliminary thinking and planning for this book began. That September, Rev. Martindale sent a memo to a number of people asking for their assistance in compiling a collection of statements by Dr. Wierwille that particularly blessed them—statements of truth, heart, wisdom, humor, and logic.

After Dr. Wierwille fell asleep in May 1985, the Board of Trustees of The Way International (Rev. Martindale; Dr. Donald E. Wierwille, Vice President; and Mr. Howard R. Allen, Secretary-Treasurer) decided that the collection of Dr. Wierwille's quotations would be compiled and published by December of 1985 and released on

December 31 in honor of Dr. Wierwille's birth
date.

The Board of Trustees asked me to oversee and
coordinate the project through its various stages.
In June, I sent a letter to every person in The Way
Corps asking each one to write down and send in
quotations by Dr. Wierwille that changed or
blessed their hearts and lives. These statements
were not to be taken from printed materials,
classes, or films; but rather from mealtime shar-
ings, personal conversations or letters, fellow-
ships, and other teaching situations. Staff of The
Way International were also asked to contribute.

By August over 2,000 quotations were sent to
me. Each was categorized and entered into our
computer to help in sorting and selecting the
quotations. The idea was not to publish an ex-
haustive collection, but to make available con-
cise quotations which would easily communicate
Dr. Wierwille's heart to a general reading audience.

I, along with Karen Wierwille Martin, Rosalie F.
Rivenbark, and Camille Kavasansky of Way
Publications, read each quotation, selected the
quotations for the book, organized them into
general topics, and recommended the visual ap-
pearance of this book for the Board of Trustees
to review. The title *Life Lines* was suggested by

Mr. Howard R. Allen and heartily endorsed by the other Trustees as an accurate description of the words of a man who spoke the Word of Life to all who would hear.

Our goal has been to make all aspects of this collection underscore the heart of the quotations—words which display Dr. Wierwille's great understanding of God and His Word, his penetrating insight into people and life, and his unique motivational ability to inspire people to move to higher planes of living.

Many people helped to produce *Life Lines*, but first of all I want to thank every person who recalled, wrote down, and sent in the quotations which moved them. Without you, there would be no book.

I'm especially thankful to the First Lady of The Way International, Mrs. Victor Paul Wierwille, for her insight and love in reviewing each quotation, as well as contributing quotations to the collection. Special acknowledgments from all of us are directed to our Board of Trustees, first, for making this project available and allowing us to be a part of it; and second, for their contributions of guidance and heart during the actual production.

Dr. Wierwille's words meant so much to each of us personally—words that still reverberate in

our minds. For us, this collection will revitalize
the significance of his statements. For those who
come to The Way Ministry after Dr. Wierwille's
departure, these words provide a dimension for
learning they could not otherwise know.

Many of the quotations will be read and enjoyed. Others will be considered deeply. Many
may be memorized and called upon over and
over again in day-by-day living, in studying, in
witnessing, and in teaching others also. None
will be lightly dismissed, because each reflects
the truth of God's Word that Dr. Wierwille lived
and taught.

In honor of the man who taught us God's
rightly divided Word, our father in the Word, we
lovingly present this book, *Life Lines: Quotations of Victor Paul Wierwille.*

Donna L. Martindale
December 1985

THE WORD OF GOD

The Word of God is the will of God.

The Bible does not contain God's Word; it is God's Word.

God's Word is the very life of God. We have life in the measure and to the extent that His Word prevails in us.

To most people the Word of God is just words; to us it is life.

When the Word of God is really living in your heart, it's like having an eagle inside, ready to burst out.

Real Life is where the reality of the Word is manifested.

If you're going to live with confidence, you've got to live with the Word.

The Word produces results; all else produces consequences.

Nothing yields greater fruit than the Word believed and practiced.

The Word is the superhighway over which our believing hauls God's mighty cargoes of truth.

Right results come from right believing from right teaching from right doctrine from right Word.

God covers every situation in life either by His Word or revelation.

The Word is never exhausted; it keeps getting bigger and bigger because you get bigger, your understanding gets bigger.

If I seek truth from sources other than God and His righteousness, I will only get ignorance. All true knowledge comes from God.

When you argue with God's Word, you get the consequences.

If you won't be humble to the Word, you will be humbled by the world.

If you are too busy to read God's Word every day, you are too busy to live.

The Word is food; it is meat; there are no poisons in it.

God's Word must be eaten, digested, and assimilated.

Once you really know the Word in a certain area, you will never hunger there again.

There are only two things you can do with God's Word—either believe it or not believe it. Nobody can break it.

Cutting up the Word will not get rid of the Author.

If the Word is not what it claims to be, the "Word of Truth," then we have no true revelation and will never really know the true God.

The master key to understanding God's Word is Jesus Christ.

Outside of Christ, there is no hope, no peace, no serenity. Outside of the Word, we have no answers.

The truth of God's Word is so simple, most people miss it a lifetime.

Read it, rightly divide it, believe it, and act on it.

The Word is more sure than the ground you walk on. This world will be gone someday, but the Word of God lives and abides forever.

Three things must constantly be recognized: (1) the absolute trustworthiness of God's Word, (2) Jesus Christ's complete and finished work, and (3) the reality of our relationship to God as sons and daughters.

No man or woman is really very strong in themselves. Men and women have to get their strength from the Word.

Circumstances will alter situations but circumstances will never alter the Word.

You put your trust in God by putting your trust in His Word.

You cannot lose anything worth having by believing God's Word.

The Word has to be built so solidly in our hearts that we become as absolutely unmovable on the Word as God Himself.

Your certainty about God's Word is the basis of your being.

Victory is determined by attitude; attitude is determined by believing; believing is determined by the Word.

The one thing the Devil doesn't want you to know is the Word.

Jesus Christ withstood the adversary with "It Is Written." That's how we also withstand that same enemy.

Wisdom is to believe what God's Word says. Error does nothing but enslave—regardless of how reasonable it may seem.

The world is filled with all kinds of glitter; it comes at you from a thousand different angles. We only come to you from one angle—the truth of the Word of God.

The Word of God is our relief, not Rolaids.

Cut out the error of the world with the scissors of the Word.

If you lose your desire for God's Word, you'll lose the Word and become enslaved by traditions of men.

Religion doesn't set men free. Only the rightly divided Word when it lives in men and prevails does that.

The Word does not bring peace, except to the believer. To others it causes trouble.

The Word is like a hammer that breaks the hardness of a soul.

The Word is a living message of a living God to men who want to live a life of abundance.

Men come and go, but the Word of God lives and abides forever.

The Word builds the urgency of the times in one's heart.

Sharing the knowledge of God's Word from generation to generation—that's the only way the Word remains alive and vigorous.

The Word of God is our only rule for faith and practice.

Hold 'er high, son.

The Word, the Word, and nothing but the Word!

BELIEVING

God calls His people "believers" because that is what He expects of them.

Believing implies obedience.

Dreams become reality for people who believe.

God is no respecter of theology, but a respecter of believing.

We must believe that believing is the key to receiving or we will never believe to receive.

Believing scales the peaks of life, climbs the highest mountains without fear.

Healing is not dependent upon whether or not you're a Christian, but whether or not you believe.

You are not healed because the pain is gone, but because the Word says so.

We've lived below par because the Word has not prevailed. We say we believe it, but we don't.

Find that promise of God...believe...and you'll receive it.

Man seldom gets around to believing God until he has exhausted all his energy trying to do it himself.

When you begin to believe what the Word says, your attitude will shake the world.

We are spiritual hitchhikers and cripples until we know the Word and act.

I can do all things by means of him who infuses inner strength into me. That attitude is the greatest attitude of success that I know.

The bolder your believing, the higher your success.

We are what we are because of our believing, not other people's believing.

I can't believe for you, but I can believe with you.

We will sink to the depths or rise to the heights of our believing.

Worry is nothing but advanced interest paid on unbelief.

You can't have a walk of believing in the Word when you continue to have condemnation.

Quit stewing about life and just believe God and His Word.

What you are doing today will determine your tomorrow.

Unbelief utters only words, not prayers.

Prayer is the living Word on the lips of believers.

If you believe when you pray, act accordingly.

Action cures fear. Nonaction strengthens fear.

The believer's fear binds the omnipotence of God.

Believing gets us out of the snare when we have been trapped by the adversary.

Every situation is our opportunity to believe God.

Think of your life as the dropping of a pebble in a pond. The prayer of one man with believing affects the whole world.

Few have realized the power of God's Word on their lips of believing.

God cannot and will not allow us to fail when we believe—because He's obligated to fulfill His Word.

God said it; that settles it. We just believe it.

SONS OF GOD

Pentecost—the spiritual shock of ages!

Nobody is outside the possibility of redemption if he will hear God's Word.

Salvation had to be free; it would be too costly for anyone to buy.

Why is grace so easy? Because it cost God so much.

When you get someone born again, you are spiritually raising that person from the dead.

Christ in me—what a reality!

The fire of the holy spirit inside you, with the Word of God, will burn the chaff in your life.

The greatest healing I know is spiritual—it's the new birth. It's spiritual, but it affects the physical.

If God is able to save to the uttermost, then God is able to heal to the uttermost.

Romans 10:9 and 10 is the greatest healing. After this comes speaking in tongues.

Speaking in tongues is our audience with God.

God wants to answer our prayers more than we want to pray them.

Speaking in tongues doesn't warm God's heart...it melts it.

You have the full proof of the rewards, the return, eternal life—all of that—every time you speak in tongues.

Speaking in tongues calms the troubled waters that are boiling inside.

If we knew how powerful speaking in tongues is, we would do it all the time.

While nothing's happening, speak in tongues.

I know no one that operates the manifestations effectually and effectively who doesn't speak in tongues much.

We must go by divine revelation rather than man's religious imagination.

If God gives you the revelation, He must have the believing in you that you can believe to carry it out.

You never strain to get revelation. All strain is drain.

You must carry out revelation literally....The greatest revelation ever given is the written Word.

The ability of God within us is limitless—how can you ever lose with that kind of Father!

One thing I want to do is make God proud of His choice.

Days of negatives and defeats are over—we are sons of God.

God sees you through the eyes of His Son who redeemed you.

Only Christ in you can take away the consciousness of sin.

The adversary's great fear is that you will know and believe your sonship rights.

A believer's delegated authority is the legal right of deliverance from all the powers of the enemy.

The believers' two major life suckers are ignorance of their legal sonship rights and self-condemnation.

The human mind can never comprehend righteousness. But the spiritual man within can absorb it, utilize it, believe it, walk on it, and bring the greatness of this truth into manifestation.

Freedom is not determined by where you are, but by who and what you are in Christ Jesus.

A millionaire acts like a millionaire because he believes the written reports of his banker, broker, and accountant. We have the written report of God's Word. And we need to claim His reports, the promises He's given us.

Hold fast—never waver on what you are in Christ Jesus.

THE INTEGRITY OF GOD'S WORD

God only has to say something once for it to be true.

If God doesn't mean what He says, then what does He mean?

The internal evidence of the Word speaks more loudly for itself than any man can speak on or in its behalf.

Don't you put a question mark where God put a period.

You'll never become convinced about the Word until you work it for yourself.

Research—not to find something new in the Word, but to establish in your own heart the inherent and inerrant accuracy of the truths of God's Word for yourself.

The truth of the Word has both immediate and ultimate profit.

Because God is behind His Word, you can no more stop the success of that Word than the sun from rising.

There is nothing in the whole universe that will nullify or invalidate one statement of God's Word.

Truth is truth, come hell or high water.

Wherever the Word is taught, if people believe it, they get results.

Faithfulness to the Word produces growth.

The greatness of the Power for Abundant Living class is not in what I say, but in the greatness behind what I say.

Truth needs no defense. All that truth needs is proclamation.

The written Word is the only reliable means of establishing accuracy and maintaining it.

The most critical of all contests is the right dividing of the Word.

Only the Word rightly divided will enable men to know God.

Accuracy can never be overdone.

The silences in God's Word, like its utterances, are full of instruction.

When and where the Word of God remains silent, he who speaks is a fool.

People question God's Word but not their stupidity about it.

Truth is forever on the scaffold.

We have no friends when it comes to the Word.

The most important thing in your life is the Word, not work.

Believers stay put. We just never budge on God's Word.

If nobody believes God's Word, it's still God's Word.

LOVE

The love of God in the renewed mind in manifestation is the badge of Christianity.

Love is a standard, an attitude to live.

Divine love makes for divine life.

The Word of God makes it possible for you to love. That's what I mean when I say the Word loves you into loving.

Love sees more, but is also willing to see less.

God loved us before we even knew what loving was.

It's a good thing God's call to love was not collect.

The mind of Christ is the key to our love life.

Some people hear with their ears; I hear with my heart.

Kids, if I were you, I'd believe for a big heart.

Anytime you walk in love, you walk out of condemnation.

You can't love others fully until you love yourself.

Take the barbed wire down around your heart.

God doesn't love on account of; He loves in spite of.

God knows all about you and still loves you.

When you forget God's grace, you will be the one to cast the first stone.

It's not how much of the Word you know, but how much love you manifest.

Where knowledge fails, heart sustains.

The great things happen in the inner chambers of the heart.

We can never afford not to love each other.

Without love there is just no joy in living. Be strong in love, kids.

Work for love's sake, not for work's sake.

It's not the amount of work you produce that's important. It's the love with which you produce it that is important and will be remembered after the gathering together.

What profit is this rightly divided Word if we don't walk in love? When you quit loving, you quit living.

Always remember, the love of God has teeth in it. You just have to know when and where to bite.

You can be dead right but dead wrong because you have no love.

Be so tender that others are tenderized by you.

There's just nobody I couldn't love and no short-comings I couldn't put up with, because God tenderized me on the inside with His love.

Love has a great amount of elasticity, but it never breaks on principle.

Two great things in marriage are love and forgiveness.

Bring up our children in the sensitivity of the love of God—that's my vision.

Only two great motivations—love or fear. All men are motivated by one or the other.

When you do something out of love and people act on it out of fear, their action is due to spiritual immaturity.

The best way to get people to love is for you to love them.

A person needs to be loved the most when he deserves to be loved the least.

I am convinced that people change slowly—at a snail's pace. Love sometimes seems to work at a snail's pace.

You can get too much criticism real quick, but you can never get too much love.

People are changed by love, not by criticism.

Love people into living.

People are to be loved, things are to be used.

You know, it's easy to bless people—all you have
to do is teach them the Word and love them.

To have love—be loving.

When a man ceases to love, he ceases to have a
purpose to live.

You can't afford not to love.

Loving someone is only one thought away.

It takes so little time and effort to love and bless
people. It's your love that has to spill over into
others' lives.

Touch is healing when it's out of the love of God.
When I touch people, I thank God for them.

The touch of someone who loves you is always healing. The touch of someone who dislikes you can be upsetting, disturbing, and shocking to the physical nervous system.

Love to serve and serve in love.

Most people get their rewards now. But you and I will receive our rewards both now and throughout all eternity because we have the heart of love.

Is there a greater giving than when God gave us His Son?

God so loved that He gave; now we must so give that others can learn to live.

RENEWED MIND

God puts in and you put on.

If God, the Creator of the heavens and the earth, isn't condemning you, then why are you condemning yourself?

If you look at yourself in the light of the Word, you'll be much more thankful.

Renewed mind believing is sanctification in manifestation.

Let your old man really die; don't just ignore him.

The only way to come out of confusion is to come back to the Word.

If you don't stay your mind, you get out of bounds.

Think about what you're thinking about.

It doesn't matter how much Word you know, success is determined by how much you put on.

Change involves work.

Most people do not use their minds but allow their minds to be used.

You only get hurt when you allow yourself to be hurt.

Get your mind off yourself and on the Word.

It isn't what you think, it is what the Word says that you should think.

Thinking patterns determine your heart.

Work the Word in your mind until your attitude is changed to the attitude of the Word.

We have to get the hurt and dirt out of our lives.

Sin makes you sick. The love of God in the renewed mind makes you well.

Get in the Word, so the Word gets in you.

Obstacles never defeat anybody; we just allow obstacles to defeat us.

In dealing with pressure, you have to realize that all pressure begins in the mind. You allow yourself to be pressured.

No situation is any more difficult than the difficulty of renewing your mind to the Word of God and walking out on it.

Talk things over with your Father. Take your shoes off and talk straight about whatever is bugging you.

When you get discouraged, you have to hide your head in God's Word until the discouragement is gone.

Change comes from the inside out.

The manifestation of what you are inside is what you do on the outside.

It is the controlling of your thinking that makes the difference between serving the true God or the adversary.

Have your mind well arranged.

A measure of a champion is how he focuses his mind.

The adversary wants to jam our mental circuits.

The more Word you drive into your heart, the more power you will have to use against the adversary.

Think what the Word says.

Why don't you be honestly positive instead of honestly negative?

What we've got to learn is to never confess a negative. When you have a problem, never tell more people than necessary.

Keep your head above negatives by filling your mind with truth.

Negatives are like mosquitoes on a blood hunt.

Positive thoughts combat negative thinking.

Be Word-conditioned, not circumstance-controlled.

We have got to keep looking up to God and quit looking down at the problem.

Be in front of need in life's situations. Put on the Word.

LIVING THE WORD

All I want to do is serve God, love people, and move the Word.

Every man is responsible before God for his believing, his walk, his sharing, his life.

If you want to be the best, then go with the best—God's the best. You can't ever be the best without Him.

You've got to think of yourself as God's best or you'll never move the Word.

You are God's masterpiece, which is the Christ in you.

The things of the past are over with; the things of the future aren't here; but the immediate present is where you have to live one day at a time, right on with God's Word.

Kids, the greatest thing in my life is to stand approved before God.

Get the vertical divine and the horizontal will be fine.

The greatness of a man's life is not measured in the material things he owns, but in the quality of life he lives according to the Word of God.

Give happily, liberally, for the joy of giving.

If you don't share out of your abundance, you will soon have no abundance to share.

When there is nothing in your life to give, there is no reason to live.

God can only give you what you are capable of receiving.

Give your best to be your best.

There may be a lot of things we as believers need to do, but let's always keep the Word first.

God's Word has to become so real to you that it's like spiritual breathing.

When the Word is the joy of your life, you will manifest the more abundant life.

Being thankful sure makes life sweeter.

The more thankful you are for what you have today, the more you'll have to be thankful for tomorrow.

Thanksgiving is thanksliving.

God has to be first in everything, not just in thought but in action.

Spend as much time studying the Word each day as you spend at the table eating and you'll grow like crazy.

The Word handles every aspect of life.

Our attitude toward the Word determines our spirituality.

Live in prayer.

God wants us to be rooted so that we're not tossed about with every wind of doctrine.

Four great words that are meaningful and powerful to those who truly want to walk: love, grace, mercy, peace.

Our first responsibility as believers is not in serving God, but in knowing Him as our heavenly Father.

When we don't rely on God to meet our need, we are sinning.

My responsibility is to accept and trust God's ability.

You will never turn the world upside down by rightly reading the Word; you'll turn it upside down by rightly living it.

You do your best. Then God will do the rest.

If you never "blew it," then you wouldn't need a savior.

The only way we can ever live with ourselves is to live with God.

When God forgives, He forgets.

The dark night of the soul or a song in the night—which way will you go?

To do the will of God is to have the blessing of God upon your life.

New songs from the heart sprout up from the soil of committed minds.

Of all the fine arts, the finest art is life. Learning to live and living life dynamically within the framework of God's Word makes life scintillating, exciting, and vivaciously enrapturing.

When we walk in the greatness of God's Word, we live life in the fast lane.

If you allow what people say or do to you to affect your decisions, you will never stand on the Word.

Don't succumb to ruts—learn to live on the high road.

We are masters of defeat, not masters in defeat.

God never made a failure. He wants people to be more than conquerors.

Meet every situation as a conqueror. We live above the world because we live in Him.

When the Lord opens the door, it swings on its own hinges. Then all you do is walk through.

Whenever you walk with God, it always profits you first.

Truly our God is a God of deliverance. He says He wishes above all things that we prosper and be in health, and He means it.

To love God is to believe the Word and act accordingly.

We need to be tough on the Word but tender in life.

Everybody is made to be recognized. God never made an unrecognized person.

The Word becomes living when I live it. The Word becomes loving when I love.

We care greatly, love immeasurably, live dynamically.

It is just as easy to think good of people as to think evil.

It is never a fight between two people; it is always a spiritual fight.

You can't go to anything or anyone but the Word, because anything else will always let you down.

When you do things, do them for the glory of God. Then you won't be disappointed.

If you are faithful, you cannot fail.

How can you be ashamed if you live God's Word?

We never said we know all the answers, but we know the One Who does.

It's really not how long we live that counts, but the quality of our lives while we are living.

Live in the Word and let the Word live in you.

PRACTICAL
COUNSEL

Your day has to start and stop with the Word.

People, you need to take time for prayer and the Word. If you're not doing this, you are too busy expending your life on second-rate causes.

Why continue to go to the world for answers when it's the world that confused you in the first place?

Read and believe the media of the Word instead of seeing, hearing, and believing the media of the world.

One must be as willing to unlearn as to learn.

To be able to change without being disturbed in your mind is an art you can learn.

The moment you begin to look back, you lose the race. It's looking unto him who is the author and finisher of our faith that enables you to win.

Looking back gives you a stiff neck.

You forget the past by continuing to build your life on the Word, not on past experiences.

Get your mind off your experiences and into the Word.

Think about tomorrow in terms of what you are doing today.

Never be satisfied with where you are—keep growing.

Don't become fossilized in systems.

Anything in the material world that keeps you from being your best for God—dump it!

Nothing is beyond our reach if we will reach beyond ourselves.

Growing is a continuous tackling of the unknown.

Never allow yourself to be grooved in the ruts of life.

Keep fluid—keep variety in your life.

You never can dream too much or believe too big.

Stay as excited about God's Word as when you first believed.

People will run your life for you unless you have the confidence to make decisions according to the Word.

Do what God tells you to do and not what people think you should do.

You only have one chance to train your children in the nurture and admonition of the lord, so do it right the first time.

Work has dignity in itself. One of the best things you can do for your kids is to teach them the joy of work.

If you ask God first, you don't need to spin your wheels.

I do one thing at a time: I may have dozens of things happening at once, but I do them one at a time. That's how I get things done.

A good deal has to be good for both parties or else it's not a good deal.

If you don't have anything good to say about someone, shut up. It's so easy to criticize, but we need to stand, fight, and believe for one another, not against each other.

Temper gets you into trouble. Pride keeps you there.

The time to correct error is at its first occurrence and as quickly as possible.

Never evaluate your life in light of others' mistakes or accomplishments.

Don't give up on God—He never gives up on you.

Never look at your inadequacy; look at God's adequacy.

Be patient with yourself.

You have to count on God above your ability or circumstances.

We are only limited to the extent that we limit the Word of God in us.

Keep that picture of Christ in you, then the job goes better.

On bad days, sometimes you just have to close shop, get the Word into your heart, and believe the sun is going to shine in the morning.

To know answers to life is to be comforted.

The only thing in the world that can heal hearts is the Word.

You can't bless anyone else until you're blessed.

Don't sacrifice your whole life just because you have a wound in one area.

Disappointments in life, yes; but never failures. We play till we win.

The key to accomplishing anything is faithfulness.

Remember, God can always make a way.

MOVING THE WORD

Better than fame or applause is the striving to further God's cause.

When Jesus Christ was raised from the dead, he immediately began witnessing.

The life of a man is worth your time.

God needs men and women who, on the spur of the moment, can hold forth the greatness of His Word with all accuracy and boldness.

If I remember what God forgave me for, I have no trouble forgiving anyone else.

People don't care what you know until they know you care.

Where the Word is sown and God is glorified, fruit is produced.

No unbeliever has anything more important to do than to listen to you speak God's Word.

Not only go where the people are, but where the people will listen.

Don't get discouraged, and don't forget to thank God and pray, okay?

Some people don't know they're hungry until you set food before them.

I've told that person the Word. Now he can never say before the judgment that he never heard the Word....I'm just glad I had the chance to tell him. Praise God.

Somebody has to plant and somebody has to water, but it takes God to give the increase.

Music must never replace the spoken Word; it just softens people to receive the Word.

It's not technique but heartbeat that will move the Word of God over the world.

No matter how many believe, someone has to speak the Word if it's going to move.

If you are in the Word, you will be sharing the Word.

People will believe the Word more than they will believe your logic, even if it's the logic of the Word. You've got to speak the Word.

Put the open Bible in front of people, otherwise they doubt your word.

When we speak God's Word, we make known His will. Then, He backs those words with His power.

It's wonderful how it is the Word and nothing but the Word that settles all the arguments for those who really want to know.

The times in which we live are more crucial than we allow ourselves to think.

If just one person stands, the Word will live.

COMMITMENT

The greatest commitment ever made is God's commitment to His Word.

You only have one life to live and give, so give your utmost for His highest.

Commitment is saying yes to the Word.

If it's to be, it's up to me.

Personal commitment is not an option; it's a necessity.

If you don't live the Word once you learn it, you will become a spiritual cripple.

History revolves around a committed few. As a result of their lives, whole civilizations change.

It doesn't take large numbers of people to make things happen; it takes a few knowledgeable and committed ones.

The steady advance of veterans is more valuable than the reckless rush of raw recruits.

True commitment means involvement.

Want a beautiful bed of roses? Bend your back and dig.

You've got to work if you expect to accomplish anything.

You will never win unless you commit yourself to something and stick to it.

If it's worth it, you must work for it.

It takes commitment to make an idea an ideal.

Whatever is required to accomplish a goal, be willing to do it.

You must be sold out to sell.

Quality is sold-out commitment.

Do each job so that you'd be proud to sign your name to it.

We have to be more sold out to our pursuit than the world is to theirs.

If you are going to succeed in anything, you must believe you are right and stick with it. Don't give up.

Successful attainment of a goal requires commitment in your soul.

People can go as far with God as they want to go.

Our great challenge is not only becoming champions, but staying champions.

If you ever discipline yourself to master an ability, you'll never lose the basics of it.

Discipline your mind to detail, not distraction.

Memory is simply caring enough to pay attention.

Your time must be disciplined or your whole life will be undisciplined.

Never allow the day to master you, you must be master of the day.

The more work you have to do, the more disciplined you have to be to get the desired work done.

It is one thing to be a winner, another thing to stay a winner.

God moves with people who move. God can move with someone who makes mistakes better than with someone who doesn't move.

You can't dwell on your weaknesses or you'll never make it to the commitment of God's Word.

There is only one word for a commandment of God—do.

Once a man truly sees the integrity of the Word, the only alternative to walking by the Word is oblivion.

People can hold the truth, but the truth won't hold them if they don't walk it.

Son, you can't wait until you're in the middle of a battle to clean your gun.

If you make up your mind about something and know it's of God—stay put. Stick it out.

We are rewarded both now and eternally for our faithfulness in this life.

The rewards of the future are God's gracious and loving heart of blessing upon those of us who remain faithful.

If I know the Word, I don't budge on it.

THE WAY TREE

Jesus Christ stood alone so we can stand in a family.

If there is no one to stand with, you still can stand; but when there is a body of believers to stand with, you need to stand with the body.

Kids, next to God and His Word, all we have is each other.

The door to the household is always open.

Be always ready to receive back with open arms those who have strayed.

Underneath are the everlasting arms of God and they have to be our arms. No one can ever sink so low but that underneath them are our arms to bring them up.

We never fully know what our prayers for each other can mean. We'll just have to wait until the return to see the video reruns.

In the household, God plays no favorites and neither should you.

Life is too short to fight.

As individuals we share, not compare.

The pressure from outside a family will be almost meaningless if that family is standing together.

At a certain point the Body of Christ becomes more than its parts.

For people to remain faithful in the household is the great strength of Christianity.

You people can't afford to be ordinary. You belong to God's royal household, born into royalty.

At one time we were spiritual paupers, but no longer!

We can live with confidence because God is our Father.

We are not poor, emaciated, weak worms of the dust. We are royalty, children of the most high God.

Throughout the ages, God had only one desire. He wanted a family. And everything He prepared He did for you, a member of His royal family.

My home is where the Word lives in the household.

The Way is His-story in the making.

There are thousands of farms in this part of the country but this is the only one that ever planted incorruptible seed and fed the world with spiritual food.

You have nothing to lose by taking Power for Abundant Living but fear.

The future of this ministry is in the children.

People, if you only knew how important you are to your grandchildren, you'd be on fire with the Word.

The only way this ministry will stand is by continuing to search the Scriptures daily.

We want God's Word in this ministry, not V.P. ministering healing every Sunday. People have to get confidence in the Word and not in a man.

All the parts of The Way Tree could be there, but unless it has the proper nourishment, there will be no fruit. This is why we have to work the Word.

The heart of The Way Twig carries the heart of the Word.

The greatness of outreach is still the effectiveness of Twig.

I'm not interested in the rapid growth of the ministry so much as I am in the solidarity with which the Word grows.

Honey, I've had people come and go, but I'm thankful for them even if they stood just for five minutes.

The Twig lives because we live the Twig.

Spontaneity—you have to have this in your Twig if you want it to be a hot Twig.

The Way Tree isn't a concrete structure; it's flexible to meet needs.

Keep the Word hot in those Twigs. The unity of purpose you share will yield a fellowship of success.

Our ministry is to build up believers to walk in the power of God.

SERVING

Jesus Christ gave himself for you; he needs you to give yourself to others.

May all your thoughts, words, and deeds abundantly serve our lord and savior, Jesus Christ.

The world is in desperate need of your life and ability.

You're totally responsible for what you do with that which God has given.

People will serve in the degree and to the capacity of their love for God.

Your "call to service" is really your serving the call.

The walk is a day-by-day reality; as you do your part for God today, God will open up unto you the way that you should go.

If you look at the task, you'll be frustrated and defeated time and time again. Anything you do, do it with a goal in mind.

Hope stimulates our endurance.

Make yourself as a believer so important in your responsibility that you just can't be dismissed. Many times great, godly accomplishments are done by people without titles.

The closer you get to God, the greater servant you will be.

God first, others second, I am willing to be third.

Born to live. Born again to serve.

If God is not my sufficiency, then service is an interruption in my plan of self-sufficiency.

I'd rather be the one taken advantage of than the one who takes advantage.

Let people walk on your feet until they can walk on their own.

We have to become spiritual eyes for people until they acquire 20/20 spiritual vision.

Put yourself into the hearts and lives of people.

Remember details so you can bless people in ways that are important to them.

God helps those who help themselves" is sheer stupidity and selfishness. It should be "God helps those who help others."

Every time you help someone overcome a fear, you are helping him become a success.

Be aware when the need is there.

When you really love God and want to serve Him, you won't care what the world says.

We must go out into the valley of human need and love with the love of God.

You can never really help people unless they will trust you with their hearts.

Love to serve and serve in love.

We've got to bless people with our lives, with our presence, with our love.

God does not regard the greatness of the work we do, but the love and tenderness with which we do it.

The greatness in life lies in giving.

You can never outgive God.

There is an unequaled satisfaction in serving God's people.

What is a man's life but to give it? What I have, I have given to you.

LEADERSHIP

The more I become a slave to the Lord Jesus Christ, the more free I become.

The greater the leader, the greater the servant.

Proverbs says a man's gift makes room for him. You make the room you want to walk in by your believing.

Attach yourself to somebody who has more ability than you—that's how you learn.

Meekness is a mark of leadership.

Honestly look at criticism. If you can learn from it, learn.

Detail is the difference between just being and being a professional.

The quality of your personal and family life reflects the quality of your life as a leader.

Greatness is dependent upon what you've got in your heart and have transferred to your head.

I'd sooner have a man with heart than just ability. Of course, heart and ability is the best, but a man with heart can go far.

Ninety percent of all failure is due to the inability to make a decision.

All life is dependent upon decision; accomplishment is attained by carrying out that decision.

It is better to make a wrong decision than to make no decision and be wrong for not making one.

The way down the ladder is faster than the way up.

Paperwork is never more important than the paperwork authored by God.

When we get so busy that we don't have time for people, that's when we work ourselves out of a job.

No one ever becomes great without the ability to believe in people.

The times I have been hurt in the ministry can't compare to the thousands of times I would have been hurt had I been in the world and not the Word.

Sometimes you have to live with a person's shortcomings in order to have his long suits.

We trust in the Lord, but we have to work with people.

In this walk of the Word, you can't look at the failures but at the successes in people's lives.

To see the Word move in our day and time, we must identify, understand, love, and be very forgiving when dealing with people.

In counseling, read them the Word. All fights are short if you have a good enough punch.

You have mastered teaching when you can teach until there are no questions left.

Teach healing when people are well—when they don't need it. Teach love when they're sick.

You can't ever teach too simply. The more simply you teach, the more sure you are that people will understand.

Teaching the Word should be like a woman's dress: long enough to cover the subject and short enough to keep it interesting.

Humor is a healing balm for people.

Teaching is an art. Most people just talk—I teach.

Let the lord do the judging after his return. You just teach the Word.

Teach everything you know. The more you teach, the more you'll receive.

You have to motivate yourself before you can motivate others.

Nothing moves without leadership.

A great leader always knows where he is going and can take his people with him.

You can't lead God's people impulsively; it takes constant preparation.

Delegating responsibility doesn't release you of responsibility.

Position has no rights or privileges when men's lives are at stake.

When a man is really walking with God, it's very difficult to find a pigeonhole to put him into.

Don't ever let spectators run your performance.

If I always did what people thought I should do, do you know where this ministry would be? Nowhere.

Any pacesetter will always be criticized, so don't worry about criticism.

When you are right at that point where you cannot do any more, then do some more—that more is always there.

Self-sacrifice is the passion of all great men.

At the core of any successful movement, there has always been a nucleus of individuals who deem the goal more important than themselves.

If no one leads, there are no followers.

So much done for so many by so few—that's leadership.

INSIGHT

Basically all life is simple for those who want it that way.

There's a simplicity about truth. Error is always complicated.

Man cannot explain God any more than the Ford can explain Henry.

Small minds talk about people; average minds talk about events; great minds talk about God's Word.

Most people don't think, they just think they think.

Ignorance is never a virtue.

If all truth is relative, then there is relatively no truth.

The media takes a lie and gets it around the world before the truth can even put its shirt on.

You can become so acclimatized to error that you think it is truth.

I believe every child has a hunger to learn about God until the world reasons it out of him.

Man is a stranger to himself until he knows God and His Word.

The sin problem is settled; only the sinner problem remains.

Many people would like to have Jesus as savior but not as lord. They want a fire escape from hell, but not a lordship for living.

You have to wake up before you stand up.

Life without aspiration has no inspiration.

Nothing in your life is so satisfying as to do the will of God.

Being out of fellowship is like being thirty feet outside the team huddle—you can't hear the quarterback's next play.

You can get lost in life more easily than in a forest.

Whatever you put your head into is what you are going to get in your head.

All of life is conditioned by words.

Action is the fruit of thought.

Ask yourself what you rejoice in and that will answer why you are where you are.

You are the sum total of the decisions you've made.

There's never an excuse for failure, but there's always a reason.

Crisis does not make character in a man; it reveals it.

Personality is what you are before people; character is what you are when you are alone with your real self.

People who do hair see hair; people who do shoes see shoes; but we who do God's Word see God's Word.

We learn to walk spiritually the same way we learn to walk physically—by walking.

To exceed an order is as disobedient as refusing to carry out an order.

Honest work is not a degradation; it is an elevation.

Selfishness—it is funny how man never fears it in himself; he only fears it in others.

The genuinely spiritual man is the offspring of unselfishness.

Material things can tie you up and slow you down spiritually.

There are two kinds of rich people: those who have lots of money and those who have no need.

God is involved in every fiber of your life and being—He's interested in all your life.

The more you invest your life in another person, the more interested you'll be in that person.

There is no good, wholesome exposure to the world you can have that will not help make the Word of God live more fully for you.

If in working the Word I never saw something new or at least something in a different light, my enthusiasm for the Word wouldn't hit the heights it does.

You rarely recognize the greatness of the moment that you're living in.

Without God and an accurate knowledge of His Word, no nation can continue to be free.

A nation is no stronger than the individual citizens who believe and speak the Word.

Wisdom is from the Lord, not necessarily from age.

Age is not a liability, but a provider of time to give you scope and understanding. In ten years you will be able to do some things in fifteen minutes that take you four hours to do now.

Age has nothing to do with learning—desire does.

Half of the joy of participation is in the anticipation.

When you recognize opportunity from the front, then you never need to view it from the back.

The faster you travel, the farther ahead you need to look.

All strain is drain.

Signs don't follow ministries; they follow believers.

The greatest cargoes of life come in over quiet seas.

A LOT OF THINGS,
KIDS...

Yeah, well...a lot of things, kids.

A lot of things go through a man's heart and life that only the man and God know.

God is so good to me, I sometimes wonder if He's mixed me up with someone else.

An athlete of the spirit is an athlete of the Word.

We are spiritual athletes and we play to win.

You'll never learn to play the game by just reading the rule book—you've got to practice it.

Don't complain to me. I didn't write the Book.

With God there is no second team. We are His first team.

We'll always win with God. Run with the Winner.

God is color-blind; He looks upon the heart.

Home is where the Word lives.

In a world full of question marks, we have the exclamation point!

I see my life far beyond today and tomorrow. I see my life from generation to generation causing the Mystery to be lived.

These are precious times, but they're very small compared to the precious times all of God's people will share throughout eternity.

Leave this life with something standing when you go.

Jesus didn't beat around the bush, he spoke to the tree.

We plant the trees so that someone else may enjoy the privilege of sitting in the shade.

This ministry is designed for men and women whose wandering days are through.

Abundance is not a state of being but a state of mind.

The key to your income is your expenses.

We will be amazed at how many rewards are given at the *bēma* for stewardship in the physical realm.

True education is preparation for living, not a means for making money.

The greatest part of education is learning to think for yourself.

If I had a team, I'd give them the cleanest, best, most pleasant dressing room. If you change the atmosphere of a building, then people's attitudes change.

I believe in you because God believed in me.

God is not in the business of spinning His wheels.

Discouragement is a sin, a trick of the adversary.

If God has called you, He won't hang up.

There's nothing too good to be true with God.

You and God make a majority.

Stay sweet, honey.

I just don't know how to teach it any better.

I wish I were the man I know to be.

God bless you. I love you. You are the best.